JOHN F. KENNEDY

ENCYCLOPEDIA of PRESIDENTS

John F. Kennedy

Thirty-Fifth President of the United States

By Zachary Kent

Consultant: Charles Abele, Ph.D.
Social Studies Instructor
Chicago Public School System

 CHILDRENS PRESS ®

CHICAGO

The Kennedys—Caroline, Jacqueline, and John—at Hyannis Port, Massachusetts

Library of Congress Cataloging-in-Publication Data

Kent, Zachary.
  John F. Kennedy.

  (Encyclopedia of presidents)
  Includes index.
  Summary: Chronicles the life and tragic death of the
man who championed foreign relations, civil rights, and
space exploration as the thirty-fifth president of the
United States.
  1. Kennedy, John F. (John Fitzgerald), 1917-1963—
Juvenile literature. 2. Presidents—United States—
Biography—Juvenile literature. [1. Kennedy, John F.
(John Fitzgerald), 1917-1963. 2. Presidents] I. Title.
II. Series.
E842.Z9K43   1987   973.922'092'4 [B] [92]   86-33441
ISBN 0-516-01390-4

Picture Acknowledgments

AP/Wide World—4, 5, 6, 11, 16, 25, 26, 27, 33,
35, 36, 40, 43, 44, 47, 50, 53, 56, 67, 69, 70, 71,
72, 75, 79, 82 (bottom), 83, 86 (bottom)

Historical Pictures Service—73, 80

John F. Kennedy Library—12, 17, 19, 21, 23
(2 photos), 28, 30, 38, 39, 41, 45, 66, 68, 87, 89

United Press International—14, 15, 48, 51, 52,
57, 58, 61, 62, 63, 64, 77, 82 (top), 84, 86 (top),
88

U.S. Bureau of Printing and Engraving—2

Cover design and illustration by
Steven Gaston Dobson

Childrens Press, Chicago
Copyright © 1987 by Regensteiner Publishing Enterprises, Inc.
All rights reserved. Published simultaneously in Canada.
Printed in the United States of America.
       10 R 96

President Kennedy delivers his inaugural address

Table of Contents

A wartime snapshot of Lieutenant Junior Grade John Fitzgerald Kennedy
in his torpedo boat, *PT 109*

Chapter 1

"They Sank My Boat"

A huge, dark object suddenly loomed out of the blackness of the South Pacific night.

"Ship at two o'clock!" shouted a startled lookout on the United States patrol, torpedo boat *PT 109*.

"Sound general quarters," ordered its skipper, Lieutenant Junior Grade John F. Kennedy. He spun his craft's wheel to meet the attack but quickly realized there was no time. Within seconds the Japanese destroyer *Amagiri* rammed the eighty-foot PT boat. The crack of splintered wood filled the air as it sliced the *109* in two. Just as swiftly the *Amagiri* sped away, leaving flaming gas slicks, wreckage, and death in the churning water behind it.

One half of the PT boat remained afloat. Of its thirteen-man crew, two were instantly crushed and drowned. In the early morning hours of August 2, 1943, Lieutenant Kennedy swam through the waters of Blackett Strait helping to gather his surviving men.

"How are you, Mac?" he asked mechanic Patrick Mac-Mahon. "I'm all right. I'm kind of burnt," groaned the badly injured sailor.

For forty-five minutes Kennedy struggled, towing Mac-Mahon to the split hulk of *PT 109*. As the light of dawn revealed their dangerous situation, Kennedy wondered what to do next.

At the start of World War II, bad health and influential family connections could have kept John F. Kennedy completely out of the military. Instead, the young patriot volunteered to join the navy and sought active service in the Solomon Islands. Now, while his stunned men gasped for breath and clung to their ruined boat, the twenty-six-year-old officer vowed to lead his crew to safety.

As the hours passed, air gurgled out of the wreck and it slowly began to sink. On the surrounding islands lurked Japanese soldiers. Soon Kennedy realized no friendly boats would come to rescue them.

"We will swim to that small island," he announced at last. He pointed to a dot of sand three miles to the southeast. No enemy would be stationed on such a tiny island, he guessed.

Swimming the breaststroke, Kennedy took a strap from MacMahon's life jacket between his teeth and towed the burned man along. A veteran of the Harvard College swimming team, Kennedy paddled strongly with Mac-Mahon floating on his back. "We're doing good," he promised the burned man each time he paused to rest. Following behind, the other crew members kept together by clinging to an eight-foot plank of wood and kicking forward through the water.

After four hours of hard work, Kennedy, MacMahon, and the others dragged themselves onto the beach of little

Plum Pudding Island. It measured only about one hundred yards across. But the sailors managed to hide themselves among its brush and palm trees.

Determined to find help, Kennedy set out that night alone. By swimming into nearby Ferguson Passage he hoped to signal a passing PT boat. The dangers of the swim were great. Coral scraped and cut his legs. A huge fish swam close to him and, afraid of sharks, he kicked his feet until it glided away. Reaching Ferguson Passage at last, Kennedy tread water for several hours but saw no PT boats. Tossed by the current and almost lost in the dark, the young lieutenant finally returned exhausted to Plum Pudding Island.

The next night Ensign George Ross repeated the attempt. But he also returned from Ferguson Passage without finding help. Desperate for food, on the third day all of the men swam to another islet half a mile away. Again Kennedy pulled Patrick MacMahon through the water tugging him along with his teeth. On Olasana Island the men cracked open a few coconuts to eat.

Still terribly hungry, the next day, August 5, Kennedy and Ross swam to neighboring Naru Island. Fearful of enemy soldiers, they crept forward as they explored this bigger island. A deserted Japanese boat lay wrecked on the coral reef near the beach. Finding a crate washed ashore, they pried it open and excitedly discovered it contained hard sugar candy. Another few feet and they uncovered a keg of water and a dugout canoe. Packing the candy and water into the canoe, Kennedy paddled back to Olasana Island to share these treasures with his crew.

The sailors on Olasana greeted him with smiles. Two friendly natives had arrived while Kennedy and Ross were away. Suddenly the men had a chance to communicate with the outside world. On the smooth side of a coconut shell the lieutenant carved a message with his sheath knife:

NAURO ISL

NATIVE KNOWS POSIT

HE CAN PILOT 11 ALIVE

NEED SMALL BOAT KENNEDY

Taking this message, the natives eagerly left on a mission to get help. Soon a British coastwatcher, A. Reginald Evans, received news of the survivors. He sent seven native scouts back to Olasana. The rice, potatoes, fish, and C rations they brought made a feast for the starving sailors. On the seventh of August the natives hid Kennedy beneath palm leaves in their canoe. Though curious Japanese planes buzzed overhead at one point, the scouts paddled Kennedy to Gomu Island. Lieutenant Evans waited there to help make rescue arrangements. As the canoe reached the sandy shore, Kennedy sat up bearded, thin, half-naked, and blotched by swelling coral wounds.

"Hello. I'm Kennedy," he thankfully announced. Though weary, Kennedy insisted on returning to Olasana Island that night on the rescue boat. Only when he saw his crew safely aboard could he completely relax at last.

Even eighteen years later, after his election as thirty-fifth president of the United States, Kennedy never forgot those difficult days in the Solomon Islands. On his Oval Office desk in the White House he kept the carved coconut shell as a constant reminder. When a high school student

Kennedy (right) and his PT crew in the South Pacific, July 1943

one day asked, "Mr. President, how did you become a war hero?" Kennedy joked, "It was absolutely involuntary. They sank my boat."

But Kennedy was a hero. Despite personal pain, with courage and leadership, he helped his crew survive its ordeal. In 1961 he brought that same unbending hope and spirit with him to the White House. A man of intelligence, wit, and charm, it was perhaps President John F. Kennedy's courage that most endeared him to the nation.

Chapter 2

Growing Pains

The second of nine children, John Fitzgerald Kennedy was born at 83 Beals Street, Brookline, Massachusetts, on May 29, 1917. The three-story wooden house can still be visited today in that Boston suburb. Though his father, Joseph P. Kennedy, never forgot the family's poor Irish Catholic roots, even in 1917 he was fast on his way to becoming rich. Tough and smart, he became the youngest bank president in the United States at the age of twenty-five. Investing in shipyards, movie theaters, and the stock market quickly made him a multimillionaire.

In spite of this success, however, Joseph Kennedy proudly claimed before all else, "My business is my family and my family is my business." Though often called away from home, he still took a strong interest in his boys and girls. Kennedy's mother, Rose, remembered, "My husband was quite a strict father; he liked the boys to win at sports and everything they tried. If they didn't win, he would discuss their failure with them, but he did not have much patience with the loser."

Opposite page: Seven-year-old John
in Brookline, Massachusetts, in 1924

Kennedy's mother, Rose, with (left to right) Joseph, Rosemary, and John

Joseph Kennedy loved all of his children, but the greatest joy of his life was his oldest son, Joseph P. Kennedy, Jr. An excellent student and a superb athlete, Joe Junior seemed a natural leader. Two years younger, John F. Kennedy, called "Jack," grew up in the shadow of his bright and outgoing brother.

As a boy, Jack was often sick. Scarlet fever nearly killed him at the age of four. In later years he came down with whooping cough, measles, chicken pox, asthma, and other painful illnesses. His mother remarked that as "a child and many times thereafter he had to spend long periods in bed, often on weekends when the others were out playing; and as a consequence he learned to love to read." Among his

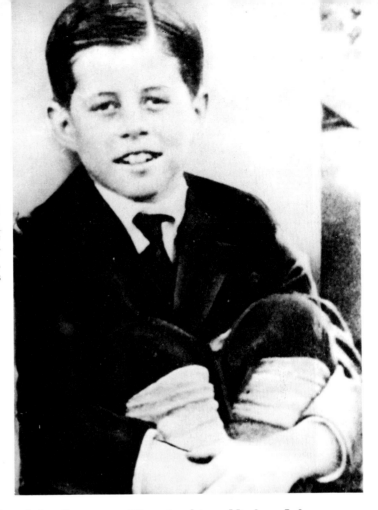

Kennedy at around the age of eight, right before he entered Dexter School in Brookline, Massachusetts

favorite childhood books were *The Arabian Nights*, John Bunyan's *Pilgrim's Progress*, and especially *King Arthur and His Knights*.

Always enthusiastic, Jack excitedly took part in outdoor activities whenever he was well. Competing with his bigger and stronger brother was difficult. When Joe and Jack had fistfights or wrestled, it was Jack who usually lost. Once the two crashed into one another during a bicycle race. As a result, Jack's bloody head required twenty-eight stitches. But Kennedys were taught never to whine or complain. If he lost a competition or was injured, Jack just tried to do better the next time.

Jack's formal education started at the private Dexter School in Brookline, but in 1926 the Kennedys moved to a big house in the suburban Riverdale section of New York City. From there Joseph Kennedy's chauffeur could easily drive the wealthy businessman to his Wall Street office. Later the family moved again a little farther north to a mansion in Bronxville, New York. Young Thomas Schriber played football with the Kennedy boys there. "There were a lot of trees around the lawn at Bronxville," he recalled years later. "I always ran looking for the trees and the ball at the same time. But Joe and Jack . . . never did, and WHANG! that was that. They were always knocking themselves out. I can remember many occasions when one or the other of the boys would be picked up unconscious; they were always bandaged and bruised all over." Living by their father's code, the Kennedys always played hard and drove themselves to win, whatever the cost.

The Kennedy family at Hyannis Port

In 1929 Joseph Kennedy bought a large white clapboard house in Hyannis Port, Cape Cod, Massachusetts. With its two-and-a-half acres of lawn and its private beach overlooking Nantucket Sound, this ten-bedroom summer cottage became the Kennedy family's truest home. His freckled face grinning, twelve-year-old Jack played tennis, learned to swim, and became an expert sailor.

"Joe and Jack were out in sailboats alone here at Hyannis Port," Joseph Kennedy bragged, "when they were so small you couldn't see their heads. It looked from the shore as if the boats were empty." In the sun and sand, with the sea breeze blowing through his hair, young Jack found in those summer days on Cape Cod some of his happiest times.

Joseph Kennedy intended that his sons receive the finest possible private school education. During fourth, fifth, and sixth grades Jack was enrolled at the Riverdale Country Day School. In 1930, at the age of thirteen, he next entered the Canterbury School in Milford, Connecticut. Fellow student Robert Sargent Shriver, Jr., Kennedy's future brother-in-law, observed that Jack was a "very wiry, energetic, peppy youngster, who played football quite well . . . despite the fact that he wasn't very heavy or physically large." Though he worried about his weight, Jack enjoyed himself there. He wrote to his parents, "We are now reading Ivanhoe in English . . . and the last time we had an exam on it I got a ninety-eight."

Unfortunately, illness struck Jack once again. In the spring of 1931 he suffered a sudden attack of appendicitis. An emergency operation forced him to rest at home the remainder of that school year.

To keep his grades up, his parents hired a tutor to help Jack during the summer. After passing English, mathematics, and Latin exams that fall, the young teenager entered Choate, a fine prep school in Wallingford, Connecticut. At Choate Jack had to compete with his older brother's established reputation. Admired by everyone, Joe eventually won the school's Harvard Trophy for his success in both scholarship and sports. Jack tried to do well at sports, too, even though he was small and thin. The coach of the Choate football team later stated, "The most burning thing I can remember about Jack was that he was a fighter. You take Joe, he was a real athlete. But Jack made up for what he lacked in athletic ability with his fight."

Jack Kennedy and some friends at Martha's Vineyard in Massachusetts

As a student Jack made no attempt to rival his brother. "I didn't work particularly hard," he admitted. His house master, John J. Maher, informed Jack's parents, ". . . he is casual and disorderly in almost all of his . . . projects. Jack studies at the last minute." Instead of doing classwork, Jack preferred winning friends with his easy sense of humor. "Joe had more personality than Jack maybe," remembered Eunice Kennedy of her older brothers, "but Jack had more charm." Choate headmaster Seymour St. John agreed. All the boys enjoyed being with Jack. "When he flashed his smile, he could charm a bird off a tree."

The most popular boys at the school all had nicknames. For a time Jack was called "Ratface." With his roommate, Lem Billings, and other friends, Jack formed the rebellious "Mucker's Club," which met nightly in his room. There the boys planned pranks and mischief. Fellow mucker Rip Horton recalled, "It was more an anti-establishment thing. Rough-housing. Sneaking out at night to get a milkshake." When the boys repeatedly broke stuffy Choate regulations, Headmaster St. John finally complained, "Well, I have two things to do, one to run the school, another to run Jack Kennedy and his friends." After receiving bad news about his son, Joseph Kennedy angrily wrote Jack, "Don't let me lose confidence in you. . . . You have the goods. Why not try to show it?"

Although he seldom received good grades, there was no question that Jack was intelligent. Lem Billings discovered with surprise that Jack received the *New York Times* at Choate. "I don't think I knew any other kid who subscribed to the New York *Times* at fourteen," he marveled, " . . . and read it every morning." Jack also read a lot of books, especially history and biography. "You would never see Jack without a book in his hand," his mother fondly remembered.

Following his graduation from Choate in 1935 Jack planned to study for a year at the London School of Economics. But in England, the eighteen-year-old came down with a serious illness called jaundice. In the fall Jack joined his friends Lem Billings and Rip Horton at Princeton University. Another attack of jaundice, however, forced him out of school after just one semester.

Kennedy on his graduation day at Choate

Hospital visits and a stay in the sunny and dry climate of Arizona gradually brought him back to health. At his father's urging, Jack entered Harvard University in the fall of 1936. When he arrived at Harvard's campus in Cambridge, Massachusetts, Jack discovered without surprise that his brother Joe had already made quite an impression there. Still a prize scholar and athlete, friends and teachers agreed that a successful future awaited Joe. It was no secret that Joseph Kennedy expected his eldest son to enter politics.

By comparison, Jack appeared careless, dreamy, and without obvious goals. To one professor Jack confessed, "Dr. Wild, I want you to know I'm not bright like my brother Joe." Rather than study hard, Jack contented himself with average grades during his first years at college.

Sports remained his greatest passion. Six feet tall but a slim 150 pounds, Jack worked hard to make the football team. "It was a matter of determination," recalled his roommate Torbert MacDonald. "After practice was over, he'd have me throw the ball for him and he'd practice snagging passes for an hour at a time, hundreds of passes." Jack made the Junior Varsity squad but a painful back injury during his sophomore year abruptly stopped his college football career.

Even illness could not keep him off the swimming team, however. Torbert MacDonald explained, "One time he had the flu, but he was set on making his letter. So every day I'd sneak into the infirmary with some food for him. As soon as he'd eaten, we'd slip out the back door, and I'd drive him to the indoor athletic building, where he'd doggedly practice his backstroke. Then I'd drive him back to the hospital. . . . Guts is the word. He had plenty of guts."

Joseph Kennedy encouraged his son to broaden his education by traveling. In the summer of 1937 Jack and Lem Billings sailed aboard the S.S. *Washington* for a long vacation in Europe. "In France," recounted Billings, "we went to every museum, every church. We brought a car over with us . . . and toured the cathedral country." Because Billings did not have a lot of money, they traveled on a strict budget. But they had a terrific time. In Italy

Scenes from Jack's
1937 trip to
Europe with his
friend Lem
Billings. Above:
Feeding pigeons in
a plaza in Venice.
Right: Jack and
Lem posing with
a little friend

they visited the Vatican and climbed to the rim of Mount Vesuvius. In Spain they watched a bullfight. "Very interesting," noted Jack, "but very cruel, especially when the bull gored the horse." Returning home, Jack excitedly described his tour. His father listened with special interest as Jack outlined the political atmosphere in Europe.

Throughout the 1930s, Joseph Kennedy's wealth, fame, and national influence had continued to grow. The terrible stock market crash of 1929 left the Kennedy fortune untouched. To clean up the dangerous practices of Wall Street traders, President Franklin Roosevelt needed a shrewd man like Joseph Kennedy. In 1934 he appointed Kennedy chairman of the powerful new Securities and Exchange Commission. In 1936, when Roosevelt ran for reelection, Kennedy lent his generous support. He even wrote a campaign book called *I'm for Roosevelt*. As a reward for his help, Roosevelt named him ambassador to Great Britain in December 1937.

With the younger children, Joseph and Rose Kennedy moved into the luxurious American Embassy in London. For the next two years Jack shuttled back and forth across the Atlantic. While visiting his family in London, he attended fancy embassy dinners and balls. Flashing his wonderful smile, Jack made a very dashing impression in his formal white tie and tails.

During his junior year in college Jack took a semester off to serve on his father's London staff. That summer of 1939 he toured Europe again, traveling to France, Italy, Poland, Latvia, Russia, Turkey, Palestine, and the Balkans. The calm atmosphere of his earlier trip seemed a distant memory. Now the continent shuddered on the verge of war. The previous year German dictator Adolf Hitler had marched his Nazi troops into Austria and Czechoslovakia. During his travels that summer of 1939, Jack sensed the Germans desired to occupy a portion of Poland also. In wild speeches Hitler whipped the German

John at work in the London embassy in 1939

people into a frenzy against Poland and its British and French allies. While driving through Berlin, Nazis pelted Jack's car with bricks because it had English license plates.

Within days of Jack's return to London, German storm troopers invaded Poland on September 1, 1939. Hurrying to Poland's defense, Great Britain and France immediately declared war on Germany. Jack soon got his first taste of World War II when a German U-boat torpedoed the British liner *Athenia* off the coast of Scotland. Ambassador Kennedy officially sent his son to Glasgow to interview American survivors of the sinking.

Finally returning to Harvard at the end of September, Jack applied himself to his studies. He proved to be an excellent student. For his senior thesis he wrote a detailed paper on England's unpreparedness for war. To his father he wrote, "Finished my thesis. . . . Am sending you a copy. . . . I'll be interested to see what you think of it, as it represents more work than I've ever done in my life."

Ambassador Joseph Kennedy and his children in London in 1939

Jack's professors gave the 150-page paper the second-highest possible grade. His father liked it so much he suggested it be made into a book. While Jack polished the manuscript, Joseph Kennedy found a publishing house eager to take it on. By late July, copies of *Why England Slept* began rolling off the printing presses. Reviewers praised the timely book. The *Boston Herald* called it "remarkable for . . . its grasp of complex problems, its courageous frankness . . . and its sound advice." Suddenly, at the age of twenty-three, Jack was a celebrated author. Excitedly he promoted the book, giving interviews on radio programs, answering letters, and autographing copies. Eventually the best-seller sold about ninety thousand copies.

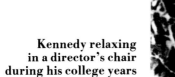
Kennedy relaxing
in a director's chair
during his college years

In London, Ambassador Kennedy was loudly insisting that the United States stay out of the war. His attitude made him so unpopular in England that President Roosevelt eventually recalled him. That summer of 1940 Jack spent time with his entire family at Hyannis Port. Charles Spaulding, a friend, stayed at the Kennedy house one weekend and never forgot the experience. Full of zest, Kennedy brothers and sisters urged their guests to sail and play touch football. "There was something doing every minute," Spaulding remarked. "The conversation at the dinner table was wonderful, lively and entertaining, ranging from the war and Washington politics to books, sports and show business. I don't think America has ever had another family quite like the Kennedys."

Chapter 3

War Hero

Having graduated from Harvard with a degree in political science, in the fall of 1940 Jack entered California's Stanford University. There he studied economics and enjoyed his fame as a writer. The war still raged in Europe, however, and Jack guessed the United States would be drawn into the fight. Early in 1941 he tried to join the army. But his old football injury caused him to fail the physical examination. All that summer Jack exercised to strengthen his bad back. In the fall he applied to the navy and managed to pass its fitness test. Then on September 22, 1941, John F. Kennedy was sworn in as an ensign.

Jack's first navy work was in the Office of Naval Intelligence. He was in Washington, D.C., on December 7, 1941, when Japanese aircraft soared down in a surprise attack on Hawaii's Pearl Harbor. Stunned and angered, the United States Congress quickly declared war on the Axis nations of Japan, Germany, and Italy. With the country suddenly plunged into the war, Jack requested active duty at sea. It would be some time, though, before he received his chance.

Opposite page: Jack in the South Pacific, 1943   29

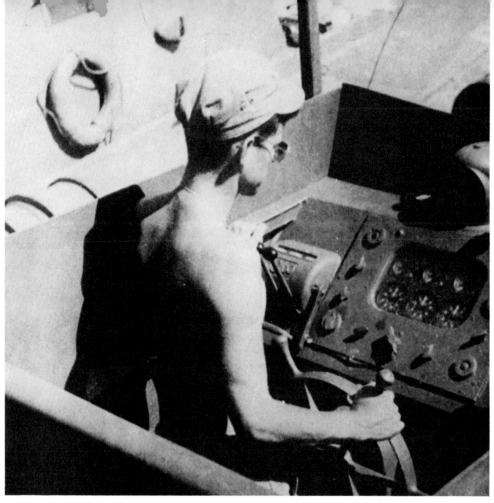

Piloting the *PT 109*

While training at the U.S. Naval Reserve Midshipman's School at Northwestern University, Kennedy first learned about PT boats. Designed to dart among the South Pacific islands, these streamlined boats could make fast, deadly attacks on heavier enemy ships. In September 1942 the navy accepted Jack into the PT school at Melville, Rhode Island. For the next six months he practiced handling a PT boat in the waters off the New England coast. He studied gunnery and navigation until he felt qualified to get into the fighting. Then he learned the navy intended to station him in a safe zone. Desperately Jack used his father's powerful connections. "They tried to ship me to Panama," he later explained, "So I called the old man and told him . . . that I wanted to see action. And the next day, just like that, the very next day, I had orders sending me off to this PT outfit in the Pacific."

Promoted by this time to lieutenant junior grade, on April 23, 1943, Kennedy took command of *PT 109*, based on Tulagi Island. For the next month the young officer whipped his boat and eleven-man crew into shape. In May the squadron moved forward to the Russell Islands ready for combat. Each night the PTs slipped deep into enemy territory on patrol. Racing home in the mornings, each PT skipper tried to reach the gas docks first.

One day Jack's desire to win caused an amusing accident. Ensign George Ross recalled, "He was going a little too fast, and the reverse gear failed, and he ploughed into the gas dock." The crash nearly tipped a dock tool shed and its occupants into the water. Sailors staggered out, shaking their fists. "How flustered the squadron commander was!" remembered Ross. "Jack could see he was about to get chewed down, and he said, 'Well, you can't stop that 109.' That got a lot of laughs."

As the Allied armed forces pushed the invading Japanese farther back, Kennedy's PT squadron established a base on Lumberi Island in the Solomons. Motoring out of Rendova Harbor, *PT 109* and its sister boats began nightly patrols around Blackett Strait. One night a Japanese plane swooped low and dropped a bomb near the *109*. Shredded metal fragments tore through the wooden craft, but fortunately no one was seriously hurt.

The damaged boat was quickly repaired, and on the evening of August 1, 1943, *PT 109* was able to make its most fateful trip to Blackett Strait. Reaching his assigned position by 9:30, Kennedy allowed his boat to idle in the water. Hour after hour the crew waited for signs of enemy ships. Simply along for the ride, Kennedy's friend Ensign Ross stood on the bow straining his eyes in the darkness. Suddenly he spotted a giant Japanese destroyer steaming at them full speed.

At the same time, Gunner Harold Marney shouted and pointed. Kennedy spun the *109*'s wheel, but its engine responded sluggishly. Almost instantly the destroyer hit and he was thrown hard across the cockpit. "This is how it feels to be killed," he thought. Knocked on his back, he watched as, inches away, the monstrous ship sheared through his boat and then quickly disappeared. Hearing the crash and seeing the burning gas tanks, other distant PT crews guessed all aboard the *109* were dead. They rushed back to Rendova Harbor to report the tragic news.

Surprisingly Kennedy, Ross, Ensign Kenny Thom, and eight enlisted men survived the *109*'s destruction. For thirty of the next thirty-six hours Kennedy remained in the water pulling Patrick MacMahon to Plum Pudding Island and seeking rescue in Ferguson Passage.

In the following days, at great personal risk, he secured food and aid for his men. On August 8 the American sailors at Rendova Harbor waved and cheered the return of the rescue PT boat that finally picked up the shipwrecked crew. Having brought his men out of danger, Jack now found himself a hero.

Kennedy proudly wears the Navy and Marine Corps Medal

To honor his bravery, the navy awarded Kennedy its Navy and Marine Corps Medal. Its citation commended his "courage, endurance and excellent leadership" which "contributed to the saving of several lives and was in keeping with the highest traditions of the United States Naval Service." The news of his adventure even made the front page of the *New York Times*.

After a needed hospital rest, Kennedy took command of another PT boat in October. On the night of November 2, 1943, *PT 59* sped to Choiseul Island and rescued sixty marines trapped by the Japanese. A few nights later the boat saw action again when it opened fire on three Japanese barges, sinking them.

In time, however, Jack's injured back began to ache terribly. Navy doctors decided he probably needed an operation. They ordered him to return to the United States for further examination. Traveling through New York City, Kennedy met a writer named John Hersey. Hearing Jack's exciting description of the loss of *PT 109*, Hersey asked for permission to write the story as a magazine article. In June 1944 the piece appeared in *The New Yorker* under the title "Survival," and later it was reprinted in the *Reader's Digest*.

At Boston's Lahey Clinic, Jack soon underwent surgery. With scalpels, doctors cut his back open and inserted a metal plate to strengthen his spine. Unfortunately the operation was not a complete success and left an open wound. At Hyannis Port, Charles Spaulding visited while Jack tried to recuperate. "That wound," observed Spaulding, "was a savage wound, a big wound. It went maybe eight inches or so down his back. It would never heal and it was open and painful. . . . I would walk up the beach with him with the back, still open, and he'd say, 'How is it now? Is it open?' or 'Is any stuff running out of it?' It was severe pain and severe discomfort." Though the wound eventually closed, Jack suffered back pain for the rest of his life.

While Jack had been fighting the war on PT boats in the South Pacific, his brother had been serving as a navy pilot in Europe. Having already completed fifty missions, on August 12, 1944, Joe Junior volunteered to fly one more. The dangerous assignment required that he guide a bomber packed with tons of explosives to an important Nazi

Lieutenant Joseph P. Kennedy, Jr., who was killed in a bomber explosion in 1944

target. Roaring forward through the sky over the English Channel, the plane suddenly exploded. Joe Kennedy and his copilot were killed instantly in the fireball.

The next day two priests arrived at Hyannis Port. Joseph Kennedy stood in shock as he learned the terrible news. Gathering the children together he told them, "I want you all to be particularly good to your mother." Then he entered his bedroom and locked the door. Every member of the family was totally stunned by the loss. For a long time that afternoon Jack sadly walked alone along the beach in front of the house.

Kennedy is showered with confetti by his campaign workers as he enters the
Boston headquarters of his 1952 Senate campaign against Henry Cabot Lodge.

Chapter 4

The Race Begins

In the spring of 1945 Nazi Germany fell in crushed defeat. The war in Europe was over at last. Discharged from the navy and with his health somewhat improved, Jack obtained a job with the Hearst newspaper chain. As a special correspondent he covered the United Nations founding conference in San Francisco, the surrender meeting at Potsdam, Germany, and the British elections. At the age of twenty-eight he seemed headed for a successful career as a newspaperman.

His father, however, pushed Jack in another direction. Later Joseph Kennedy explained, "I got Jack into politics; I was the one. I told him Joe was dead and that it was therefore his responsibility to run for Congress. He didn't want to. He felt he didn't have the ability. . . . But I told him he had to."

"It was like being drafted," Jack revealed to a friend. "My father wanted his eldest son in politics. 'Wanted' isn't the right word. He *demanded* it. You know my father." "My brother Joe was the logical one in the family to be in politics," he admitted, "and if he had lived, I'd have kept on being a writer."

Kennedy campaigning for Congress in 1946—Above: Chatting with Boston longshoremen Opposite page: Speaking before a community group

Instead, he chose to run for Congress in 1946. Years earlier, Jack's grandfather, John "Honey Fitz" Fitzgerald, had served as mayor of Boston. Now Jack entered the Democratic primary race in the Eleventh Massachusetts Congressional District, which covered parts of Boston and neighboring communities. Touring the area Kennedy observed the district's simple, hard-working longshoremen handling freight along the waterfront. Quietly he revealed, "These are the kind of people I want to represent."

Most friends agreed Jack lacked the skills of a natural politician. Campaign worker Mark Dalton remarked, "Deep down, he was an aggressive person, but he was always shy." "He was never a polished public speaker at that time," remembered navy buddy Jim Reed. Having made his decision, however, Jack threw himself into the race with every ounce of his energy.

Joseph Kennedy never forgot seeing his son campaign for the first time. "I was in Maverick Square in East Boston, talking with a man I knew. . . . I looked across the street and saw Jack get out of a car. He walked up to a bunch of hard-boiled guys standing on the corner, put his hand out and introduced himself, asking for their vote. . . . I never thought Jack had it in him."

The effect of Jack's shy, honest, manner of speaking greatly impressed campaign worker Dave Powers. One night Kennedy addressed a group of Gold Star Mothers, women who had lost sons during World War II. Powers noticed that as Jack tried to bring his talk to an end, "he sort of stammered and stuttered for a while; then he looked out at them, and, coming from the heart—you could feel it—he said, 'I think I know how you mothers feel, because my mother is a Gold Star Mother too.' " Smiling with tears in their eyes, the women crowded around the handsome young man. Powers overheard them saying, "He reminds me of my own Mike or John or Dan."

A 1946 campaign appearance

Clearly Jack possessed great personal appeal. But with nine other candidates competing for the nomination, he understood the need to campaign hard. Dave Powers described a typical day of campaigning. "He would stand outside the Charlestown Navy Yard from seven to eight o'clock, shaking thousands of workmen's hands as they went in the gate." Through the rest of the morning he walked the neighborhood streets knocking on every door and introducing himself. After gulping a hurried lunch, Powers remembered, "In the afternoon, we'd stop on the main street, at the barbershops and the variety stores and the taverns." They also visited the local fire houses and police stations. Then at four o'clock Kennedy returned to the Navy Yard to greet workers at another gate. In the evening he attended five or six house parties where he could meet small groups of voters.

Kennedy (second from left) with fellow PT-boat veterans

Loyal friends and family members gathered in Boston to help Jack in any way they could. Navy pals and Choate and Harvard schoolmates wrote speeches, offered legal advice, and passed out pamphlets door to door. Twenty-year-old Robert Kennedy campaigned for his brother in East Cambridge. Eunice Kennedy worked in the Boston campaign office. Even fourteen-year-old Teddy Kennedy lent his support by fetching supplies and coffee. Jack's mother, Rose Kennedy, held successful tea parties for women voters. At the first one, a thousand women jammed into a Cambridge hotel, eager for a chance to meet and chat with the candidate.

Wearing a green tie, Jack marched in Boston's Saint Patrick's Day parade. Financed by his father's money, posters announcing "Kennedy for Congress" appeared throughout the district. Before he was finished Jack made some 450 speeches. At one rally, after listening to the chairman introduce one candidate after another as "a young fellow who came up the hard way," Jack finally stepped forward and joked, "I seem to be the only person here tonight who didn't come up the hard way!" Though he tried not to make his wealth a campaign issue, he honestly claimed, "I have an obligation as a rich man's son to people who are having a hard time of it."

Primary election day arrived at last on June 17, 1946. Anxiously Jack waited to hear the results, but he need not have worried. When the votes were tallied it was announced Kennedy received nearly twice as many votes as his nearest competitor.

Kennedy had no difficulty winning the general election against his Republican opponent in November. The people of the Eleventh District were mostly Democrats. On January 3, 1947, in Washington, D.C., he raised his right hand and took the oath of office of a United States congressman.

At thirty years of age, Jack's handsomely boyish looks made him appear much younger. During one of his first days in the House of Representatives he was mistaken for a House page and asked to run an errand. Even in 1948 at a rally for President Truman, Secret Service men refused to believe he was a congressman. "Yeah, that's Congressman Kennedy," vouched a rally official who called over to identify him.

Congressman Kennedy marching in Boston's Bunker Hill Parade in 1949

Kennedy installed himself in a comfortable apartment in the Georgetown area of Washington. A cook and a valet kept his home life in order. During his early years in Congress he enjoyed Washington social life as a popular, carefree bachelor.

At the Capitol the young representative went to work trying to help the citizens of his Massachusetts district. Many veterans just back from the war needed places to live. Kennedy introduced a bill calling for federal money to pay for low-cost housing. While working on the Education and Labor Committee he met another young congressman named Richard Nixon. The two sat together, remembered Nixon, "like a pair of unmatched bookends." Kennedy liked the California Republican and even contributed to Nixon's campaign when he ran for the Senate in 1950.

Kennedy and Adlai Stevenson (waving), campaigning in Boston in 1952

Kennedy himself was easily reelected to Congress in 1948 and 1950. As time passed, however, he found his position frustrating. A member of the House of Representatives lacked the power to do the things Jack wished to do. As 1952 approached, Kennedy decided to run for the United States Senate.

In preparation for the campaign he hung a map of Massachusetts on the wall of his Boston apartment. Pins marked the places he had visited since the last election. He was determined to speak in every city and town in Massachusetts before the people voted again. To Dave Powers he insisted, "You've got to get me some dates here, here, and there. When we've got this map completely covered with pins . . . I'll announce my candidacy."

Kennedy shakes hands with his opponent, Henry Cabot Lodge.

By the spring of 1952 the map was full of pins and Kennedy openly began his campaign, proclaiming, "Other states have vigorous leaders in the United States Senate to defend the interest and principles of their citizens. . . . Massachusetts has need for such leadership." The man Kennedy challenged, Republican Henry Cabot Lodge, was very popular in Massachusetts and important nationally. With typical determination Kennedy set out to beat this powerful opponent.

Again he received tremendous help from friends and family. Dave Powers remembered how hard the Kennedy sisters—Eunice, Pat, and Jean—worked. "When they campaigned in Framingham, they knocked on every door in town. If someone was out when they knocked on the door, they'd go back the next morning." Rose Kennedy and her daughters hosted thirty-five tea parties attended by more than sixty thousand women. Laboring night and day throughout the race, Robert Kennedy served as his brother's campaign manager.

Jack Kennedy's father provided extremely valuable financial aid. "It takes three things to win in politics," claimed Joseph Kennedy. "The first is money, the second is money, and the third is money." When the *Boston Post* threatened to support Lodge, Joseph Kennedy secretly loaned the needy newspaper $500,000 and his son got the endorsement instead.

For eight months Jack Kennedy traveled back and forth across the state, living on cheeseburgers and milk shakes. Often his aching back required that he use crutches. Before entering a crowded hall to speak, he would hand them to Dave Powers to keep hidden out of sight. Sometimes he stood on receiving lines for hours while suffering throbbing back pain. But he knew he had to make the effort if he were going to win. By election night campaign worker Francis Morrissey proudly claimed, "I'll bet he talked to at least a million people and shook hands with 750,000."

All the sacrifice and hard work paid off. In a surprising upset, Kennedy beat Lodge by 70,737 votes. Completely stunned, Lodge reportedly muttered, "It was those damn tea parties that beat me." But, of course, it was much more than that. Learning of his victory, an exhausted Jack Kennedy thanked his campaign workers and then announced, "Now I'm going home to bed."

Opposite page: Kennedy and Adlai Stevenson

John Kennedy and his brother Robert (left) at the Senate Rackets Committee
hearings in 1957. Robert was counsel for the committee and John was a member.

Chapter 5

A Profile in Courage

In Washington the new young senator from Massachusetts caused a bit of a sensation. Rich, charming, and handsome with his penetrating gray eyes and dazzling smiles, all his life Kennedy had no trouble getting dates. Now women recognized him as the most eligible bachelor in the United States. Some sat in the Senate gallery just to watch him and hear him speak.

A friend of Kennedy's, Charles Bartlett, knew a young woman he thought would be Kennedy's perfect match. At a dinner party he introduced him to Jacqueline Lee Bouvier. "Jackie" was working as a newspaper photographer at the *Washington Times Herald*. Observing her at dinner, Kennedy was struck by her beauty, poise, and intelligence. Later he teasingly recalled, "I leaned over the asparagus and asked her for a date."

Over the next months the two began a romance. They casually went to the movies or dinner, but Kennedy also escorted her to President Eisenhower's inaugural ball. In the spring of 1953 Jacqueline traveled to England to write pieces on Queen Elizabeth II's coronation for her newspaper. Kennedy soon sent her a telegram: ARTICLES EXCELLENT, BUT YOU ARE MISSED. Finally he made a transatlantic telephone call and asked her to marry him.

Senator Kennedy and his bride, Jacqueline Lee Bouvier Kennedy, after their wedding

The news of their engagement made all the society pages. Soon after the two made a visit to Hyannis Port, *Life* magazine recorded the event. With photographs of the couple sailing near Cape Cod, the article was entitled: "*Life* Goes Courting with a US Senator."

On September 12, 1953, thirty-six-year-old John F. Kennedy and twenty-four-year-old Jacqueline Bouvier were married in a huge Roman Catholic ceremony. At least six thousand people crowded outside the Church in Newport, Rhode Island, hoping to glimpse the happy newlyweds. At the invitation of Jackie's wealthy step-

Three Kennedy brothers confer: Robert, Ted, and John

father, Hugh Auchincloss, twelve hundred guests attended the wedding reception at his Hammersmith Farm estate.

Settling into married life, Jackie began preparing a home for them, while Jack Kennedy returned to his work as a United States senator. At the risk of angering Massachusetts shipping interests, he supported the Saint Lawrence Seaway project. The *Boston Post* accused him of "ruining New England." But Kennedy believed the increased commerce traveling through that improved waterway would greatly benefit the entire nation even if it slightly hurt New England.

Making a point at the McCarthy hearings. Left to right: Committee members Robert Kennedy, John McClellan, and Joseph McCarthy

Another delicate matter required Kennedy to walk a political tightrope. During the late 1940s, the Soviet Union forced its harsh Communist influence over Eastern Europe. In China, Mao Tse-tung led a Communist revolution. Suddenly a worldwide threat of Communism worried many Americans. By the early 1950s Wisconsin Senator Joe McCarthy and other congressmen warned of Communists hiding in the United States. At Senate hearings McCarthy hounded innocent citizens as he publicly searched for Communists in both the government and industry. For a time this "Red Scare" seized the minds of Americans. Gradually, however, people realized McCarthy was exceeding the powers of his office. As the nation calmed down, Jack Kennedy watched, unwilling to commit himself, while others criticized his old friend.

Kennedy, with Jackie, leaving the New York hospital where he underwent back surgery

Through the summer of 1954, Kennedy's back hurt him so much that he needed his crutches constantly. Doctors recommended against another dangerous back operation. Kennedy, however, slapped his crutches and responded, "I'd rather be dead than spend the rest of my life on these things." On October 10 he entered the New York Hospital for Special Surgery. In the operating room a medical team labored for hours fusing spinal disks in their patient's back. But the operation proved a failure, and when an infection soon set in, Kennedy slipped into a coma. For a time, while family and friends prayed for him, he seemed very close to death.

Only after a few frightening days did he reopen his eyes and begin to rally. By February 1955 he had grown well enough to allow doctors to operate again. The new surgery involved the removal of the metal plate supporting his spine and a replacement bone graft. This more successful procedure required a long and difficult period of healing afterwards.

Kennedy was flown to his parents' home in Palm Beach, Florida, to recuperate. Jackie stayed close by his side performing all the duties of a loving nurse. While flat on his back in bed Jack still took care of his business as a senator. He read mail and dictated letters. "Afternoons," he stated, "I talk by telephone with the office."

To fill other empty hours he decided to write a book. "Politics is a jungle," he scribbled in his notes. A politician is "torn between doing the right thing and staying in office . . . between the local interest and the national interest . . . between the private good . . . and the general good." In *Profiles in Courage* Kennedy wrote short biographies of eight United States senators, including John Quincy Adams, Daniel Webster, and Sam Houston. These men had all shown special political courage by supporting unpopular causes. They had risked their careers by standing up for what they felt was right. Though staff members helped him with the research and editing of this important book, Kennedy wrote the manuscript himself. In May 1955 Harper & Row accepted the book for publication.

Kennedy returned at last to Washington and the Senate, though he still experienced discomfort. "At least half the days that he spent on this earth were days of intense physical pain," remarked Robert Kennedy. But he added, "I never heard him complain." Required to wear a corset back brace under his clothes at all times, he entered the Senate chamber smiling. Announced the *New York Herald Tribune*, "Jack Kennedy comes from a bold and sturdy breed, and he's back on the job again."

In the summer of 1955 the senator traveled to Europe. A visit to Warsaw, "to make a study of conditions in Communist Poland," increased his reputation as an expert on foreign affairs. When *Profiles in Courage* went on sale in bookstores in 1956, it added to his prestige. Americans snatched up the well-written book and read it avidly. "This is a great book that every student of government — in fact every voter should read," advised the *Oregon Journal*. As his fame and popularity blossomed, Kennedy cast his eye upon the approaching presidential contest of 1956.

In June, excited Democratic delegates packed the International Amphitheatre in Chicago to choose a presidential candidate. Former Illinois Governor Adlai Stevenson had waged a losing race in 1952 against Republican Dwight D. Eisenhower. "We're madly for Adlai," chanted throngs of convention delegates, calling for his renomination. Clearly Stevenson was their choice again for 1956. While the crowd waved banners and cheered, John F. Kennedy gave a stirring speech putting Stevenson's name in nomination. With the vice-presidential position still up for grabs, impressed listeners thought Kennedy might be perfect for that spot. But other powerful politicians also competed for the post. Though he could have chosen his own running mate, Stevenson allowed the delegates to choose.

Kennedy leading
Stevenson supporters
at the Democratic
National Convention

In the balloting that followed, Kennedy seemed a strong contender. Many delegations supported the popular young senator. During the second ballot vote, Senator Lyndon Johnson announced that all fifty-six Texas votes would go to "that fighting senator who wears the scars of battle . . . John Kennedy of Massachusetts." By the third ballot, however, the voting suddenly swung to Senator Estes Kefauver of Tennessee. "That's it—let's go," grimly remarked Kennedy as he watched the final results on his hotel room television. He walked to the convention hall and gave a generous speech supporting Kefauver.

In November President Eisenhower and his running mate, Richard Nixon, completely overwhelmed Stevenson and Kefauver in the general election. As the Democratic Party tried to pull itself together, Jack Kennedy began to think about his future. When a Democrat suggested Kennedy could run for vice-president again in 1960, he re-

Chapter 6

Let's Back Jack!

On January 2, 1960, a crush of reporters filled the Senate Caucus Room. At noon John F. Kennedy stepped up to a microphone and formally stated, "I am announcing today my candidacy for the presidency of the United States." Immediately people made an issue of Kennedy's youthfulness. Senator Lyndon Johnson, who also wanted to be president, insisted the country needed someone "with a touch of gray in his hair." In private, President Eisenhower referred to Kennedy as "that boy."

"Do you think a forty-two-year-old can meet the demands made on the president?" questioned a reporter. He did not realize the senator had just had a birthday.

"I don't know about a forty-two-year-old," smiled Kennedy, "but I think a forty-three-year-old can."

Kennedy's strategy to win the nomination was simple but difficult. "Every primary has to be won," he insisted to his staff. Crisscrossing the country in an airplane, he began his tireless campaign battle to secure votes in the primary states. "I married a whirlwind," marveled Jacqueline. "He's indestructible. People who try to keep up with him drop like flies, including me."

In New Hampshire, Wisconsin, and West Virginia, Kennedy picked up startling victories. Shaking voters' hands until his own grew blistered, giving speeches until hoarseness forced him to rest, Kennedy scored successes in many other states as well. His energy and earnest hope for a brighter future won the admiration of many Democrats.

That July, when the 1960 Democratic National Convention opened in Los Angeles, Kennedy possessed 600 of the needed 761 delegate votes. In the state-by-state balloting that followed, other delegations quickly jumped on the Kennedy bandwagon. He was short by only thirteen votes when the counting reached Wyoming's fifteen-vote delegation. Excitedly its leader shouted his announcement. "Wyoming casts all fifteen votes for the next president of the United States, John Kennedy!" A band blared "Happy Days Are Here Again" and cheers rang out as Kennedy reached the podium to thank the convention. On the first ballot he had won the Democratic nomination.

Soon after, Kennedy received a message from his chief convention rival, Lyndon Baines Johnson. "LBJ," Johnson wrote, referring to his initials, "now means Let's Back Jack." Recognizing the Texan's tremendous political strength, Kennedy offered him the vice-presidential spot.

On July 15, 1960, eighty thousand Democrats jammed into the Los Angeles Coliseum to hear their candidate's acceptance speech. "We stand on the edge of a New Frontier," Kennedy exclaimed, "the frontier of the 1960s. . . . Beyond that frontier are uncharted areas of science and space, unsolved problems of peace and war, unconquered pockets of ignorance and prejudice,

Kennedy and Johnson in Los Angeles, waiting to make their acceptance speeches

unanswered questions of poverty and surplus." In taking
on these challenges, Kennedy called upon Americans to be
"new pioneers of that New Frontier."

In Chicago, Republicans met to nominate their candidates. For president they picked Vice-President Richard
Nixon and welcomed Henry Cabot Lodge of Massachusetts
to be his running mate. Familiar with both of these men,
Kennedy prepared for a tough campaign.

Through the following days the candidates traveled the
country speaking to the people. As a Roman Catholic,
many Americans worried that Kennedy's religious beliefs
would interfere with his decisions as president. In answer
Kennedy asked, "Did forty million Americans lose their
right to run for the presidency on the day they were bap-
tized as Catholics?" To a group of Protestant ministers he
urged, "judge me on the basis of my record of fourteen
years in Congress. . . . I do not speak for my church on
public matters—and the church does not speak for me."

Kennedy and Nixon debate before a television audience of millions.

The greatest excitement of the campaign occurred when Kennedy and Nixon met in four television debates. Kennedy studied hard to prepare for these confrontations, spending hours flipping through index cards of facts. Obviously tan and handsome, he displayed calm confidence during the debates. By contrast, under the glaring television studio lights, Nixon seemed pale and nervous.

On the day of the election, November 8, 1960, opinions remained so evenly divided that pollsters could not predict which candidate would win. After voting in Boston Kennedy flew to Hyannis Port to watch the unfolding results that evening on television with family and friends. As the state returns were reported, the contest seesawed back and forth. Kennedy won in some states but was losing in others. Mayor Richard Daley of Chicago telephoned to predict: "With a little bit of luck and the help of a few close friends, you're going to carry Illinois." It was rumored old Joseph Kennedy had spread a lot of money in that state.

Chapter 7

The New Frontier

On the freezing, snowy day of January 20, 1961, thousands of Americans stood shoulder to shoulder near the Capitol to witness Kennedy's inauguration. Black opera star Marian Anderson sang "The Star-Spangled Banner" and Vermont poet Robert Frost recited a special poem. At 12:51 in the afternoon, Supreme Court Chief Justice Earl Warren administered the oath of office. Swearing to uphold the laws of the Constitution, John F. Kennedy became the first Roman Catholic United States president and the first president born in the twentieth century.

Coatless in the blistering cold, Kennedy turned and faced the crowd. In a ringing inaugural address he proclaimed, "Let the word go forth from this time and place, to friend and foe alike, that the torch has been passed to a new generation of Americans . . . tempered by war, disciplined by a hard and bitter peace, proud of our ancient heritage. . . . Let every nation know, whether it wishes us well or ill, that we shall pay any price, bear any burden . . . to assure the survival and the success of liberty." The difficulties of the nation, Kennedy warned, required the help of every citizen. "And so, my fellow Americans," he challenged, "ask not what your country can do for you; ask what you can do for your country."

Opposite page: Kennedy's own handwritten notes
for his famous inaugural address

65

The swearing-in ceremony for Kennedy's cabinet members

Enthusiastically Kennedy, often called "JFK" by the press, took up his first duties in the White House. As secretary of state he chose Dean Rusk, and for secretary of defense Robert McNamara. Other important cabinet posts and advisory positions were filled by the best thinkers Kennedy could find. People soon laughed that no professors would be left to teach in America's Ivy League colleges when the president was through. For the post of attorney general he picked his brother Robert. In response to complaints, Kennedy explained that he wanted the best man possible for the job, "and they don't come any better than Bobby."

A Peace Corps worker in Colombia supervises farmers making bricks.

Immediately Kennedy's "New Frontier" administration began programs to insure freedom throughout the world. On March 1, 1961, he signed an executive order creating the Peace Corps, to be headed by his brother-in-law Sargent Shriver. Soon, idealistic Peace Corps volunteers were offering their knowledge to needy countries. In jungle villages and among desert huts, they helped dig wells and plant crops. Kennedy also extended the United States foreign aid program. Every day cargo ships full of food steamed into the harbors of Asia's and Africa's starving nations. In addition his Alliance for Progress program strengthened ties with Latin America.

Kennedy on the White House porch with Caroline, John-John, and Macaroni

At home Americans found themselves thrilled by Kennedy's swift energy and charming style. They enjoyed Kennedy's witty responses to questions during the nation's first live televised news conferences. They also got used to hearing his unusual Boston accent. "What's wrong with the American fah-mer today?" he once asked a crowd in Iowa. "He's stah-ving," yelled a farmer in the audience. Everyone, including Kennedy, loudly laughed.

"The pay is good and I can walk to work," Kennedy often joked about his job. With his attractive young family he made the White House his comfortable home. Little Caroline Kennedy, born in 1957, often rode her pet pony,

The president in his rocking chair

Macaroni, on the White House lawn. Her baby brother, John Kennedy, Jr., called John-John, loved to romp in the Oval Office while his father worked. To ease his bad back, Kennedy often rested in a rocking chair. In constant motion, Kennedy's rocker became a symbol of his presidency.

If Jack Kennedy impressed people with his vigor, beautiful Jackie Kennedy was admired for her sense of culture. After redecorating the White House with historic furniture and art, she took Americans on a fascinating televised tour. Fashion-conscious women tried to copy the clothes Jackie wore. Her round "pillbox" hats, as well as her sleeveless formal gowns, set trends across the country.

**Cuban prisoners captured by
Fidel Castro's militia**

Immediate problems faced Kennedy during his first few months in office. Ninety miles from the coast of Florida, Communists under the command of revolutionary Fidel Castro had grabbed control of the island of Cuba in 1959. Soon after, America's Central Intelligence Agency put a secret plan in motion. In a mountain camp in Guatemala, fourteen hundred Cuban exiles received military training. These men hoped to return to Cuba and overthrow Castro's government. After consulting his military experts and CIA advisers, Kennedy allowed the plan to proceed. On April 17, 1961, American boats landed the anti-Castro brigade on the beaches of Cuba's Bay of Pigs. From the start, however, the Bay of Pigs invasion proved a complete disaster. Outnumbered 143 to 1, the beaten soldiers of the little army threw up their hands in surrender.

The total failure of the mission shocked Kennedy. For a time his worldwide image as a leader suffered. "Victory has a hundred fathers and defeat is an orphan," he quietly stated. Instead of shifting the blame to his advisers, Kennedy took full responsibility for the foolish adventure.

Opposite page: At Camp David, Maryland, Kennedy discusses the Cuban Missile Crisis with former President Dwight D. Eisenhower.

Top: Astronauts Alan Shepard, Virgil Grissom, Gordon Cooper
Bottom: Walter Schirra, Donald Slayton, John Glenn, Scott Carpenter

Kennedy's many dealings with the Soviet Union presented him with opportunities to rebuild his prestige. On April 11, 1961, Soviet Major Yuri Gagarin became the first human to rocket into space. Determined to keep pace with the Soviets, Kennedy eagerly promoted the United States space exploration program. On May 5, 1961, Alan Shepard became the first American launched into space, and in the next two years other brave astronauts followed. Americans cheered John Glenn as a national hero after his space capsule made three orbits of the earth in 1962. Astronauts Virgil Grissom, Scott Carpenter, Walter Schirra, and Gordon Cooper all advanced America's position in the space race during other early flights. Looking to the

Meeting in Vienna: American President Kennedy, Soviet Premier Nikita Khrushchev, and Soviet Foreign Minister Andrei Gromyko

future, Kennedy told Congress, "I believe that this nation should commit itself to achieving the goal, before the decade is out, of landing a man on the moon and returning him safely to earth." In 1969 Kennedy's incredible dream came true when Neil Armstrong and Edwin Aldrin first stepped upon the moon.

To calm world tensions, Kennedy recognized the importance of meeting Soviet Premier Nikita Khrushchev face-to-face. On June 3, 1961, Kennedy arrived in Vienna, Austria, where the two world leaders held informal talks. During their discussions, however, they seemed to disagree on every issue. In an attempt to bully Kennedy, Khrushchev raged that Communist revolutions would soon spring up throughout the world.

Later Kennedy noticed a medal pinned on Khrushchev's chest. "That's the Lenin Peace Prize," proudly revealed the Russian. In a soft voice Kennedy told him, "I hope they let you keep it." Returning to the United States, Kennedy publicly admitted the failure of the meetings. "No spectacular progress," he told Americans, "was either achieved or pretended."

One event that soon threatened relations between the two nations was the construction of the Berlin Wall in August 1961. Since World War II Germany's capital had been jointly occupied by United States and Soviet troops. In time, large numbers of Germans began crossing from Communist controlled East Berlin to democratic West Berlin. To halt this increasing flow, the Communists suddenly ordered the building of a twenty-five mile wall across the middle of the city. With concrete and barbed wire, thousands of laborers finished the task in four short days. Closely guarded, this Berlin Wall prevented other East Germans from ever reaching freedom.

To meet the threat to peace, Kennedy rushed more American soldiers into West Berlin. In June 1963 he traveled to the city to bolster the spirits of the cut-off East Berliners. With the ugly wall at his back, Kennedy addressed hundreds of thousands of excited listeners.

"There are many people in the world," he exclaimed, "who really don't understand, or say they don't, what is the great issue between the free world and the Communist world. Let them come to Berlin. . . . Freedom has many difficulties and democracy is not perfect but we have never had to put up a wall to keep our people in."

From an observation platform, Kennedy looks across the Berlin Wall into East Berlin.

A sea of German faces roared their approval of these words. They yelled even louder when Kennedy finally told them, "All free men, wherever they may live, are citizens of Berlin, and therefore, as a free man, I take pride in the words: *"Ich bin ein Berliner!"* ("I am a Berliner!")

In that thrilling moment the troubled city became a shining symbol of liberty throughout the world, and Kennedy scored perhaps the greatest triumph of his personal career. The greatest test of Kennedy's leadership, however, had occurred several months earlier.

On the morning of October 16, 1962, presidential assistant McGeorge Bundy interrupted Kennedy's bedroom breakfast with bad news. "Mr. President, there is now hard photographic evidence . . . that the Russians have offensive missiles in Cuba." Flying high over Cuba, American U-2 spy planes had snapped pictures of nuclear missile bases under construction. Millions of Americans could face the danger of speedy and direct nuclear attack.

Immediately Kennedy called together a group of his closest advisers. "This is the week when I had better earn my salary," he told former secretary of state Dean Acheson. For several tense days the president and the executive committee of the National Security Council secretly studied their options. Some advisers wanted to bomb the Cuban missile sites. Other committee members pushed for a navy blockade of the island instead.

Finally Kennedy announced his decision: "It's going to be a blockade." That night he revealed the situation to the American people. In a televised speech he vowed, "All ships of any kind bound for Cuba will, if found to contain cargoes of offensive weapons, be turned back." He also demanded that the Cuban missile bases be dismantled.

At 10:00 on the morning of October 24 the U.S. naval blockade went into effect. American aircraft carriers and destroyers, 180 boats in all, formed a chain across the Caribbean Sea five hundred miles from the Cuban coast.

Within minutes several Soviet freighters loomed upon the horizon. As these ships drew closer and closer the danger of war suddenly seemed very real. Americans waited breathlessly to see if the Soviets would try to force their way through.

At 10:25 Kennedy and his advisers learned crucial news. John McCone, director of the CIA, announced that some of the Soviet ships had "stopped dead in the water." Others were turning and moving away.

Greatly relieved, Secretary of State Rusk smiled and said, "We're eyeball to eyeball and I think the other fellow just blinked."

A U.S. destroyer inspects a Soviet freighter carrying suspicious cargo to Cuba.

Several days of difficult negotiations remained, but the Soviets had shown their unwillingness to provoke a confrontation. On October 28 Premier Khrushchev even agreed to dismantle the missiles already in Cuba. "In . . . the cause of peace," his official declaration read, "the Soviet government . . . has given a new order . . . to crate and return them to Soviet Russia."

Taking advantage of the moment, Kennedy urged that the two nations stop their dangerous tests of atomic weapons in the atmosphere. In the following months the United States and the Soviet Union arranged for the signing of an important nuclear test ban treaty. Also at Kennedy's suggestion, a direct telephone line was installed between the White House and the Kremlin in Moscow. In the event of any future emergency, the president and the Soviet premier could talk immediately on this "hot line."

As relations calmed somewhat between the two countries, Kennedy turned to deal with a problem closer to home. After suffering years of shameful treatment as second-class citizens, America's blacks were rising and demanding their civil rights. Banding together in the Deep South, blacks refused to obey unfair state laws and challenged segregation practices that kept them separate from whites. Under the leadership of the Reverend Martin Luther King, Jr., blacks marched the streets of cities such as Jackson, Mississippi, and Montgomery, Alabama.

Resentful southern whites responded with terrible violence. Under murderous attack, peaceful marches often turned into deadly riots. During a protest in Birmingham, Alabama, police rushed among black marchers. They swung nightsticks, beating defenseless people bloody. High-pressure fire hoses were sprayed across the crowd, knocking people down. Barking police dogs nipped the legs of running women and tore the clothes of children. Throughout the South in the early 1960s, these sad scenes were repeated again and again.

America's blacks, however, continued to insist upon their rights. In 1962 the United States Supreme Court ordered that James Meredith be granted admission into the all-white University of Mississippi. In answer, angry mobs threatened the black man's life. To insure Meredith's safety and to keep the peace during his first days of enrollment, Kennedy ordered National Guardsmen to the Oxford, Mississippi, campus. As brave and hopeful blacks registered at other southern schools, Kennedy sent protective federal troops to those colleges as well.

Chapter 8

An Eternal Flame

At the age of forty-six and nearing the end of his third year as president, Kennedy began to plan his campaign to run for a second term. On Friday November 22, 1963, he flew with his wife to Dallas, Texas, as part of a political tour. Thousands of cheering Texans lined the long route that brought the presidential motorcade from Love Field Airport into the city. Smiling and waving, the Kennedys sat in an open limousine with Texas governor John B. Connally and his wife.

At about 12:30 in the afternoon the car drove past a large brick building called the Texas School Book Depository. Turning in her seat, Mrs. Connally pleasantly remarked to the president, "You certainly can't say that the people of Dallas haven't given you a nice welcome." Before he had time to answer her, from a sixth-floor window of the book warehouse, the sudden crack of a rifle shattered the day's joyful atmosphere. Kennedy pitched forward as a bullet struck him in the neck. Almost instantly a second shot pierced Governor Connally's body, seriously wounding him. Before people understood what was happening, a third and final bullet crashed through the back of Kennedy's skull.

Above: President and Mrs. Kennedy passing through downtown Dallas
Below: Kennedy slumps against his wife as a bullet strikes him in the head.

Lyndon B. Johnson takes the oath of office in the cabin of the presidential plane.

"Jack! Oh no! No!" cried Jacqueline Kennedy, clutching her husband against her.

Stunned witnesses watched as Secret Service agent Clinton Hill jumped onto the back of the limousine to offer protection. Jacqueline Kennedy reached back and helped him climb to the seats. "The president has been shot!" shouted a voice into a police radio. Sirens screamed as a police motorcycle escort rushed the car through the Dallas streets to Parkland Memorial Hospital.

Though doctors worked frantically to save Kennedy's life, there was little they could do. At 1:00, reporters hurried from the hospital to spread the horrible news. John F. Kennedy was dead, the victim of an assassination.

In dazed confusion, hospital workers placed the body in a bronze coffin. At 2:38, aboard the presidential plane, Vice-President Lyndon Johnson took the oath of office as president of the United States. Beside him in the crowded cabin stood Jacqueline Kennedy, her dress and stockings still covered with her husband's blood.

Jack Ruby shoots Lee Harvey Oswald two days after Kennedy's assassination.

Within hours of Kennedy's death, Dallas police handcuffed the man they believed responsible for the murder. They claimed Lee Harvey Oswald, an ex-Marine and Communist sympathizer, had also killed Dallas police officer J. D. Tippit while escaping from the crime scene. "I haven't shot anybody!" yelled Oswald to the police.

He would never live to stand trial. Two days later, while Oswald was being transferred to county jail, a Dallas nightclub owner named Jack Ruby elbowed his way past policemen and news camera crews. Shocked Americans watched live on television as Ruby shouted, "You killed the president, you rat!" He drew a concealed pistol and fired point-blank into Oswald's body. Though a presidential commission headed by Chief Justice Earl Warren would later find Lee Harvey Oswald guilty of President Kennedy's death, many unanswered questions and suspicions would forever surround the awful event.

In the days following the assassination, Americans reacted with the greatest possible sadness. In fact, millions of people throughout the world behaved as though they had lost a personal friend. In cities and towns on every continent, people wept upon hearing the tragic news. Candlelight vigils were held and many streets and public buildings were renamed in Kennedy's honor.

In Washington, after lying in state in the East Room of the White House and later in the Capitol rotunda, the day arrived on Monday, November 25, for Kennedy's funeral. Across the country millions of grieving Americans watched the ceremony on television. After a funeral Mass at Saint Matthew's Cathedral, a military honor guard lifted the flag-draped coffin onto a wooden gun carriage. Dressed in black, Jacqueline Kennedy bravely stood on the steps of the church with her children. In a touching gesture few Americans would ever forget, three-year-old John Kennedy, Jr., raised his hand in a farewell salute to his father.

In a long and somber procession, six white horses drew the caisson through the streets of Washington. Muffled drums beat a mournful march for escorting military companies. Behind the coffin a soldier led a single riderless black horse. The empty boots reversed in its stirrups symbolized the nation's terrible loss. Farther behind, presidents, kings, and diplomats from all over the world followed in silent tribute.

Past dipped flags and weeping spectators, the solemn parade wound its way across the Potomac River. "He belongs to the country," Jacqueline Kennedy had decided,

**Above: Mrs. Kennedy and Caroline pray beside the president's casket in the Capitol rotunda.
Below: The procession crosses Memorial Bridge on the way to Arlington National Cemetery.**

World leaders and other dignitaries look on as the flag is folded over Kennedy's casket.

and so on a hill overlooking the capital, among the graves of other military veterans, servicemen lowered Kennedy's casket into the ground at Arlington National Cemetery. In the blue sky overhead, fifty-one planes roared past, representing the fifty states and the president. While twenty-one rifles were shot in final salute, the folded coffin flag was presented to the president's widow.

A guard stands before the eternal flame in Arlington National Cemetery.

John F. Kennedy was gone, but his energy and courage would never be forgotten. Beside his grave an eternal flame was lit as a lasting symbol of the spirit and dreams he impressed upon his countrymen. "Ask not what your country can do for you," he had challenged, "ask what you can do for your country," and perhaps his greatest mission for Americans was expressed in the speech he intended to give that tragic day in Dallas. "We in this country, in this generation," the words remind us, "are—by destiny rather than choice—the watchmen on the walls of world freedom. We ask, therefore, that we may be worthy of our power and responsibility—that we may exercise our strength with wisdom and restraint—and that we may achieve in our time and for all time the ancient vision of peace on earth, good will toward men."

Opposite page: John F. Kennedy, Jr., salutes a final farewell to his father.

Chronology of American History

(Shaded area covers events in John F. Kennedy's lifetime.)

About A.D. 982—Eric the Red, born in Norway, reaches Greenland in one of the first European voyages to North America.

About 1000—Leif Ericson (Eric the Red's son) leads what is thought to be the first European expedition to mainland North America; Leif probably lands in Canada.

1492—Christopher Columbus, seeking a sea route from Spain to the Far East, discovers the New World.

1497—John Cabot reaches Canada in the first English voyage to North America.

1513—Ponce de Léon explores Florida in search of the fabled Fountain of Youth.

1519-1521—Hernando Cortés of Spain conquers Mexico.

1534—French explorers led by Jacques Cartier enter the Gulf of St. Lawrence in Canada.

1540—Spanish explorer Francisco Coronado begins exploring the American Southwest, seeking the riches of the mythical Seven Cities of Cibola.

1565—St. Augustine, Florida, the first permanent European town in what is now the United States, is founded by the Spanish.

1607—Jamestown, Virginia, is founded, the first permanent English town in the present-day U.S.

1608—Frenchman Samuel de Champlain founds the village of Quebec, Canada.

1609—Henry Hudson explores the eastern coast of present-day U.S. for the Netherlands; the Dutch then claim parts of New York, New Jersey, Delaware, and Connecticut and name the area New Netherland.

1619—The English colonies' first shipment of black slaves arrives in Jamestown.

1620—English Pilgrims found Massachusetts's first permanent town at Plymouth.

1621—Massachusetts Pilgrims and Indians hold the famous first Thanksgiving feast in colonial America.

1623—Colonization of New Hampshire is begun by the English.

1624—Colonization of present-day New York State is begun by the Dutch at Fort Orange (Albany).

1625—The Dutch start building New Amsterdam (now New York City).

1630—The town of Boston, Massachusetts, is founded by the English Puritans.

1633—Colonization of Connecticut is begun by the English.

1634—Colonization of Maryland is begun by the English.

1636—Harvard, the colonies' first college, is founded in Massachusetts. Rhode Island colonization begins when Englishman Roger Williams founds Providence.

1638—Delaware colonization begins as Swedes build Fort Christina at present-day Wilmington.

1640—Stephen Daye of Cambridge, Massachusetts prints *The Bay Psalm Book*, the first English-language book published in what is now the U.S.

1643—Swedish settlers begin colonizing Pennsylvania.

About 1650—North Carolina is colonized by Virginia settlers.

1660—New Jersey colonization is begun by the Dutch at present-day Jersey City.

1670—South Carolina colonization is begun by the English near Charleston.

1673—Jacques Marquette and Louis Jolliet explore the upper Mississippi River for France.

1682—Philadelphia, Pennsylvania, is settled. La Salle explores Mississippi River all the way to its mouth in Louisiana and claims the whole Mississippi Valley for France.

1693—College of William and Mary is founded in Williamsburg, Virginia.

1700—Colonial population is about 250,000.

1703—Benjamin Franklin is born in Boston.

1732—George Washington, first president of the U.S., is born in Westmoreland County, Virginia.

1733—James Oglethorpe founds Savannah, Georgia; Georgia is established as the thirteenth colony.

1735—John Adams, second president of the U.S., is born in Braintree, Massachusetts.

1737—William Byrd founds Richmond, Virginia.

1738—British troops are sent to Georgia over border dispute with Spain.

1739—Black insurrection takes place in South Carolina.

1740—English Parliament passes act allowing naturalization of immigrants to American colonies after seven-year residence.

1743—Thomas Jefferson is born in Albemarle County, Virginia. Benjamin Franklin retires at age thirty-seven to devote himself to scientific inquiries and public service.

1744—King George's War begins; France joins war effort against England.

1745—During King George's War, France raids settlements in Maine and New York.

1747—Classes begin at Princeton College in New Jersey.

1748—The Treaty of Aix-la-Chapelle concludes King George's War.

1749—Parliament legally recognizes slavery in colonies and the inauguration of the plantation system in the South. George Washington becomes the surveyor for Culpepper County in Virginia.

1750—Thomas Walker passes through and names Cumberland Gap on his way toward Kentucky region. Colonial population is about 1,200,000.

1751—James Madison, fourth president of the U.S., is born in Port Conway, Virginia. English Parliament passes Currency Act, banning New England colonies from issuing paper money. George Washington travels to Barbados.

1752—Pennsylvania Hospital, the first general hospital in the colonies, is founded in Philadelphia. Benjamin Franklin uses a kite in a thunderstorm to demonstrate that lightning is a form of electricity.

1753—George Washington delivers command that the French withdraw from the Ohio River Valley; French disregard the demand. Colonial population is about 1,328,000.

1754—French and Indian War begins (extends to Europe as the Seven Years' War). Washington surrenders at Fort Necessity.

1755—French and Indians ambush Braddock. Washington becomes commander of Virginia troops.

1756—England declares war on France.

1758—James Monroe, fifth president of the U.S., is born in Westmoreland County, Virginia.

1759—Cherokee Indian war begins in southern colonies; hostilities extend to 1761. George Washington marries Martha Dandridge Custis.

1760—George III becomes king of England. Colonial population is about 1,600,000.

1762—England declares war on Spain.

1763—Treaty of Paris concludes the French and Indian War and the Seven Years' War. England gains Canada and most other French lands east of the Mississippi River.

1764—British pass the Sugar Act to gain tax money from the colonists. The issue of taxation without representation is first introduced in Boston. John Adams marries Abigail Smith.

1765—Stamp Act goes into effect in the colonies. Business virtually stops as almost all colonists refuse to use the stamps.

1766—British repeal the Stamp Act.

1767—John Quincy Adams, sixth president of the U.S. and son of second president John Adams, is born in Braintree, Massachusetts. Andrew Jackson, seventh president of the U.S., is born in Waxhaw settlement, South Carolina.

1769—Daniel Boone sights the Kentucky Territory.

1770—In the Boston Massacre, British soldiers kill five colonists and injure six. Townshend Acts are repealed, thus eliminating all duties on imports to the colonies except tea.

1771—Benjamin Franklin begins his autobiography, a work that he will never complete. The North Carolina assembly passes the "Bloody Act," which makes rioters guilty of treason.

1772—Samuel Adams rouses colonists to consider British threats to self-government.

1773—English Parliament passes the Tea Act. Colonists dressed as Mohawk Indians board British tea ships and toss 342 casks of tea into the water in what becomes known as the Boston Tea Party. William Henry Harrison is born in Charles City County, Virginia.

1774—British close the port of Boston to punish the city for the Boston Tea Party. First Continental Congress convenes in Philadelphia.

1775—American Revolution begins with battles of Lexington and Concord, Massachusetts. Second Continental Congress opens in Philadelphia. George Washington becomes commander-in-chief of the Continental army.

1776—Declaration of Independence is adopted on July 4.

1777—Congress adopts the American flag with thirteen stars and thirteen stripes. John Adams is sent to France to negotiate peace treaty.

1778—France declares war against Great Britain and becomes U.S. ally.

1779—British surrender to Americans at Vincennes. Thomas Jefferson is elected governor of Virginia. James Madison is elected to the Continental Congress.

1780—Benedict Arnold, first American traitor, defects to the British.

1781—Articles of Confederation go into effect. Cornwallis surrenders to George Washington at Yorktown, ending the American Revolution.

1782—American commissioners, including John Adams, sign peace treaty with British in Paris. Thomas Jefferson's wife, Martha, dies. Martin Van Buren is born in Kinderhook, New York.

1784—Zachary Taylor is born near Barboursville, Virginia.

1785—Congress adopts the dollar as the unit of currency. John Adams is made minister to Great Britain. Thomas Jefferson is appointed minister to France.

1786—Shays's Rebellion begins in Massachusetts.

1787—Constitutional Convention assembles in Philadelphia, with George Washington presiding; U.S. Constitution is adopted. Delaware, New Jersey, and Pennsylvania become states.

1788—Virginia, South Carolina, New York, Connecticut, New Hampshire, Maryland, and Massachusetts become states. U.S. Constitution is ratified. New York City is declared U.S. capital.

1789—Presidential electors elect George Washington and John Adams as first president and vice-president. Thomas Jefferson is appointed secretary of state. North Carolina becomes a state. French Revolution begins.

1790—Supreme Court meets for the first time. Rhode Island becomes a state. First national census in the U.S. counts 3,929,214 persons. John Tyler is born in Charles City County, Virginia.

1791—Vermont enters the Union. U.S. Bill of Rights, the first ten amendments to the Constitution, goes into effect. District of Columbia is established. James Buchanan is born in Stony Batter, Pennsylvania.

1792—Thomas Paine publishes *The Rights of Man*. Kentucky becomes a state. Two political parties are formed in the U.S., Federalist and Republican. Washington is elected to a second term, with Adams as vice-president.

1793—War between France and Britain begins; U.S. declares neutrality. Eli Whitney invents the cotton gin; cotton production and slave labor increase in the South.

1794—Eleventh Amendment to the Constitution is passed, limiting federal courts' power. "Whiskey Rebellion" in Pennsylvania protests federal whiskey tax. James Madison marries Dolley Payne Todd.

1795—George Washington signs the Jay Treaty with Great Britain. Treaty of San Lorenzo, between U.S. and Spain, settles Florida boundary and gives U.S. right to navigate the Mississippi. James Polk is born near Pineville, North Carolina.

1796—Tennessee enters the Union. Washington gives his Farewell Address, refusing a third presidential term. John Adams is elected president and Thomas Jefferson vice-president.

1797—Adams recommends defense measures against possible war with France. Napoleon Bonaparte and his army march against Austrians in Italy. U.S. population is about 4,900,000.

1798—Washington is named commander-in-chief of the U.S. Army. Department of the Navy is created. Alien and Sedition Acts are passed. Napoleon's troops invade Egypt and Switzerland.

1799—George Washington dies at Mount Vernon, New York. James Monroe is elected governor of Virginia. French Revolution ends. Napoleon becomes ruler of France.

1800—Thomas Jefferson and Aaron Burr tie for president. U.S. capital is moved from Philadelphia to Washington, D.C. The White House is built as presidents' home. Spain returns Louisiana to France. Millard Fillmore is born in Locke, New York.

1801—After thirty-six ballots, House of Representatives elects Thomas Jefferson president, making Burr vice-president. James Madison is named secretary of state.

1802—Congress abolishes excise taxes. U.S. Military Academy is founded at West Point, New York.

1803—Ohio enters the Union. Louisiana Purchase treaty is signed with France, greatly expanding U.S. territory.

1804—Twelfth Amendment to the Constitution rules that president and vice-president be elected separately. Alexander Hamilton is killed by Vice-President Aaron Burr in a duel. Orleans Territory is established. Napoleon crowns himself emperor of France. Franklin Pierce is born in Hillsborough Lower Village, New Hampshire.

1805—Thomas Jefferson begins his second term as president. Lewis and Clark expedition reaches the Pacific Ocean.

1806—Coinage of silver dollars is stopped; resumes in 1836.

1807—Aaron Burr is acquitted in treason trial. Embargo Act closes U.S. ports to trade.

1808—James Madison is elected president. Congress outlaws importing slaves from Africa. Andrew Johnson is born in Raleigh, North Carolina.

1809—Abraham Lincoln is born near Hodgenville, Kentucky.

1810—U.S. population is 7,240,000.

1811—William Henry Harrison defeats Indians at Tippecanoe. Monroe is named secretary of state.

1812—Louisiana becomes a state. U.S. declares war on Britain (War of 1812). James Madison is reelected president. Napoleon invades Russia.

1813—British forces take Fort Niagara and Buffalo, New York.

1814—Francis Scott Key writes "The Star-Spangled Banner." British troops burn much of Washington, D.C., including the White House. Treaty of Ghent ends War of 1812. James Monroe becomes secretary of war.

1815—Napoleon meets his final defeat at Battle of Waterloo.

1816—James Monroe is elected president. Indiana becomes a state.

1817—Mississippi becomes a state. Construction on Erie Canal begins.

1818—Illinois enters the Union. The present thirteen-stripe flag is adopted. Border between U.S. and Canada is agreed upon.

1819—Alabama becomes a state. U.S. purchases Florida from Spain. Thomas Jefferson establishes the University of Virginia.

1820—James Monroe is reelected. In the Missouri Compromise, Maine enters the Union as a free (non-slave) state.

1821—Missouri enters the Union as a slave state. Santa Fe Trail opens the American Southwest. Mexico declares independence from Spain. Napoleon Bonaparte dies.

1822—U.S. recognizes Mexico and Colombia. Liberia in Africa is founded as a home for freed slaves. Ulysses S. Grant is born in Point Pleasant, Ohio. Rutherford B. Hayes is born in Delaware, Ohio.

1823—Monroe Doctrine closes North and South America to European colonizing or invasion.

1824—House of Representatives elects John Quincy Adams president when none of the four candidates wins a majority in national election. Mexico becomes a republic.

1825—Erie Canal is opened. U.S. population is 11,300,000.

1826—Thomas Jefferson and John Adams both die on July 4, the fiftieth anniversary of the Declaration of Independence.

1828—Andrew Jackson is elected president. Tariff of Abominations is passed, cutting imports.

1829—James Madison attends Virginia's constitutional convention. Slavery is abolished in Mexico. Chester A. Arthur is born in Fairfield, Vermont.

1830—Indian Removal Act to resettle Indians west of the Mississippi is approved.

1831—James Monroe dies in New York City. James A. Garfield is born in Orange, Ohio. Cyrus McCormick develops his reaper.

1832—Andrew Jackson, nominated by the new Democratic Party, is reelected president.

1833—Britain abolishes slavery in its colonies. Benjamin Harrison is born in North Bend, Ohio.

1835—Federal government becomes debt-free for the first time.

1836—Martin Van Buren becomes president. Texas wins independence from Mexico. Arkansas joins the Union. James Madison dies at Montpelier, Virginia.

1837—Michigan enters the Union. U.S. population is 15,900,000. Grover Cleveland is born in Caldwell, New Jersey.

1840—William Henry Harrison is elected president.

1841—President Harrison dies in Washington, D.C., one month after inauguration. Vice-President John Tyler succeeds him.

1843—William McKinley is born in Niles, Ohio.

1844—James Knox Polk is elected president. Samuel Morse sends first telegraphic message.

1845—Texas and Florida become states. Potato famine in Ireland causes massive emigration from Ireland to U.S. Andrew Jackson dies near Nashville, Tennessee.

1846—Iowa enters the Union. War with Mexico begins.

1847—U.S. captures Mexico City.

1848—John Quincy Adams dies in Washington, D.C. Zachary Taylor becomes president. Treaty of Guadalupe Hidalgo ends Mexico-U.S. war. Wisconsin becomes a state.

1849—James Polk dies in Nashville, Tennessee.

1850—President Taylor dies in Washington, D.C.; Vice-President Millard Fillmore succeeds him. California enters the Union, breaking tie between slave and free states.

1852—Franklin Pierce is elected president.

1853—Gadsden Purchase transfers Mexican territory to U.S.

1854—"War for Bleeding Kansas" is fought between slave and free states.

1855—Czar Nicholas I of Russia dies, succeeded by Alexander II.

1856—James Buchanan is elected president. In Massacre of Potawatomi Creek, Kansas-slavers are murdered by free-staters. Woodrow Wilson is born in Staunton, Virginia.

1857—William Howard Taft is born in Cincinnati, Ohio.

1858—Minnesota enters the Union. Theodore Roosevelt is born in New York City.

1859—Oregon becomes a state.

1860—Abraham Lincoln is elected president; South Carolina secedes from the Union in protest.

1861—Arkansas, Tennessee, North Carolina, and Virginia secede. Kansas enters the Union as a free state. Civil War begins.

1862—Union forces capture Fort Henry, Roanoke Island, Fort Donelson, Jacksonville, and New Orleans; Union armies are defeated at the battles of Bull Run and Fredericksburg. Martin Van Buren dies in Kinderhook, New York. John Tyler dies near Charles City, Virginia.

1863—Lincoln issues Emancipation Proclamation: all slaves held in rebelling territories are declared free. West Virginia becomes a state.

1864—Abraham Lincoln is reelected. Nevada becomes a state.

1865—Lincoln is assassinated in Washington, D.C., and succeeded by Andrew Johnson. U.S. Civil War ends on May 26. Thirteenth Amendment abolishes slavery. Warren G. Harding is born in Blooming Grove, Ohio.

1867—Nebraska becomes a state. U.S. buys Alaska from Russia for $7,200,000. Reconstruction Acts are passed.

1868—President Johnson is impeached for violating Tenure of Office Act, but is acquitted by Senate. Ulysses S. Grant is elected president. Fourteenth Amendment prohibits voting discrimination. James Buchanan dies in Lancaster, Pennsylvania.

1869—Franklin Pierce dies in Concord, New Hampshire.

1870—Fifteenth Amendment gives blacks the right to vote.

1872—Grant is reelected over Horace Greeley. General Amnesty Act pardons ex-Confederates. Calvin Coolidge is born in Plymouth Notch, Vermont.

1874—Millard Fillmore dies in Buffalo, New York. Herbert Hoover is born in West Branch, Iowa.

1875—Andrew Johnson dies in Carter's Station, Tennessee.

1876—Colorado enters the Union. "Custer's last stand": he and his men are massacred by Sioux Indians at Little Big Horn, Montana.

1877—Rutherford B. Hayes is elected president as all disputed votes are awarded to him.

1880—James A. Garfield is elected president.

1881—President Garfield is assassinated and dies in Elberon, New Jersey. Vice-President Chester A. Arthur succeeds him.

1882—U.S. bans Chinese immigration. Franklin D. Roosevelt is born in Hyde Park, New York.

1884—Grover Cleveland is elected president. Harry S. Truman is born in Lamar, Missouri.

1885—Ulysses S. Grant dies in Mount McGregor, New York.

1886—Statue of Liberty is dedicated. Chester A. Arthur dies in New York City.

1888—Benjamin Harrison is elected president.

1889—North Dakota, South Dakota, Washington, and Montana become states.

1890—Dwight D. Eisenhower is born in Denison, Texas. Idaho and Wyoming become states.

1892—Grover Cleveland is elected president.

1893—Rutherford B. Hayes dies in Fremont, Ohio.

1896—William McKinley is elected president. Utah becomes a state.

1898—U.S. declares war on Spain over Cuba.

1900—McKinley is reelected. Boxer Rebellion against foreigners in China begins.

1901—McKinley is assassinated by anarchist Leon Czolgosz in Buffalo, New York; Theodore Roosevelt becomes president. Benjamin Harrison dies in Indianapolis, Indiana.

1902—U.S. acquires perpetual control over Panama Canal.

1903—Alaskan frontier is settled.

1904—Russian-Japanese War breaks out. Theodore Roosevelt wins presidential election.

1905—Treaty of Portsmouth signed, ending Russian-Japanese War.

1906—U.S. troops occupy Cuba.

1907—President Roosevelt bars all Japanese immigration. Oklahoma enters the Union.

1908—William Howard Taft becomes president. Grover Cleveland dies in Princeton, New Jersey. Lyndon B. Johnson is born near Stonewall, Texas.

1909—NAACP is founded under W.E.B. DuBois

1910—China abolishes slavery.

1911—Chinese Revolution begins. Ronald Reagan is born in Tampico, Illinois.

1912—Woodrow Wilson is elected president. Arizona and New Mexico become states.

1913—Federal income tax is introduced in U.S. through the Sixteenth Amendment. Richard Nixon is born in Yorba Linda, California. Gerald Ford is born in Omaha, Nebraska.

1914—World War I begins.

1915—British liner *Lusitania* is sunk by German submarine.

1916—Wilson is reelected president.

1917—U.S. breaks diplomatic relations with Germany. Czar Nicholas of Russia abdicates as revolution begins. U.S. declares war on Austria-Hungary. John F. Kennedy is born in Brookline, Massachusetts.

1918—Wilson proclaims "Fourteen Points" as war aims. On November 11, armistice is signed between Allies and Germany.

1919—Eighteenth Amendment prohibits sale and manufacture of intoxicating liquors. Wilson presides over first League of Nations; wins Nobel Peace Prize. Theodore Roosevelt dies in Oyster Bay, New York.

1920—Nineteenth Amendment (women's suffrage) is passed. Warren Harding is elected president.

1921—Adolf Hitler's stormtroopers begin to terrorize political opponents.

1922—Irish Free State is established. Soviet states form USSR. Benito Mussolini forms Fascist government in Italy.

1923—President Harding dies in San Francisco, California; he is succeeded by Vice-President Calvin Coolidge.

1924—Coolidge is elected president. Woodrow Wilson dies in Washington, D.C. James Carter is born in Plains, Georgia. George Bush is born in Milton, Massachusetts.

1925—Hitler reorganizes Nazi Party and publishes first volume of *Mein Kampf*.

1926—Fascist youth organizations founded in Germany and Italy. Republic of Lebanon proclaimed.

1927—Stalin becomes Soviet dictator. Economic conference in Geneva attended by fifty-two nations.

1928—Herbert Hoover is elected president. U.S. and many other nations sign Kellogg-Briand pacts to outlaw war.

1929—Stock prices in New York crash on "Black Thursday"; the Great Depression begins.

1930—Bank of U.S. and its many branches close (most significant bank failure of the year). William Howard Taft dies in Washington, D.C.

1931—Emigration from U.S. exceeds immigration for first time as Depression deepens.

1932—Franklin D. Roosevelt wins presidential election in a Democratic landslide.

1933—First concentration camps are erected in Germany. U.S. recognizes USSR and resumes trade. Twenty-First Amendment repeals prohibition. Calvin Coolidge dies in Northampton, Massachusetts.

1934—Severe dust storms hit Plains states. President Roosevelt passes U.S. Social Security Act.

1936—Roosevelt is reelected. Spanish Civil War begins. Hitler and Mussolini form Rome-Berlin Axis.

1937—Roosevelt signs Neutrality Act.

1938—Roosevelt sends appeal to Hitler and Mussolini to settle European problems amicably.

1939—Germany takes over Czechoslovakia and invades Poland, starting World War II.

1940—Roosevelt is reelected for a third term.

1941—Japan bombs Pearl Harbor, U.S. declares war on Japan. Germany and Italy declare war on U.S.; U.S. then declares war on them.

1942—Allies agree not to make separate peace treaties with the enemies. U.S. government transfers more than 100,000 Nisei (Japanese-Americans) from west coast to inland concentration camps.

1943—Allied bombings of Germany begin.

1944—Roosevelt is reelected for a fourth term. Allied forces invade Normandy on D-Day.

1945—President Franklin D. Roosevelt dies in Warm Springs, Georgia; Vice-President Harry S. Truman succeeds him. Mussolini is killed; Hitler commits suicide. Germany surrenders. U.S. drops atomic bomb on Hiroshima; Japan surrenders: end of World War II.

1946—U.N. General Assembly holds its first session in London. Peace conference of twenty-one nations is held in Paris.

1947—Peace treaties are signed in Paris. "Cold War" is in full swing.

1948—U.S. passes Marshall Plan Act, providing $17 billion in aid for Europe. U.S. recognizes new nation of Israel. India and Pakistan become free of British rule. Truman is elected president.

1949—Republic of Eire is proclaimed in Dublin. Russia blocks land route access from Western Germany to Berlin; airlift begins. U.S., France, and Britain agree to merge their zones of occupation in West Germany. Apartheid program begins in South Africa.

1950—Riots in Johannesburg, South Africa, against apartheid. North Korea invades South Korea. U.N. forces land in South Korea and recapture Seoul.

1951—Twenty-Second Amendment limits president to two terms.

1952—Dwight D. Eisenhower resigns as supreme commander in Europe and is elected president.

1953—Stalin dies; struggle for power in Russia follows. Rosenbergs are executed for espionage.

1954—U.S. and Japan sign mutual defense agreement.

1955—Blacks in Montgomery, Alabama, boycott segregated bus lines.

1956—Eisenhower is reelected president. Soviet troops march into Hungary.

1957—U.S. agrees to withdraw ground forces from Japan. Russia launches first satellite, *Sputnik.*

1958—European Common Market comes into being. Fidel Castro begins war against Batista government in Cuba.

1959—Alaska becomes the forty-ninth state. Hawaii becomes fiftieth state. Castro becomes premier of Cuba. De Gaulle is proclaimed president of the Fifth Republic of France.

1960—Historic debates between Senator John F. Kennedy and Vice-President Richard Nixon are televised. Kennedy is elected president. Brezhnev becomes president of USSR.

1961—Berlin Wall is constructed. Kennedy and Khrushchev confer in Vienna. In Bay of Pigs incident, Cubans trained by CIA attempt to overthrow Castro.

1962—U.S. military council is established in South Vietnam.

1963—Riots and beatings by police and whites mark civil rights demonstrations in Birmingham, Alabama; 30,000 troops are called out, Martin Luther King, Jr., is arrested. Freedom marchers descend on Washington, D.C., to demonstrate. President Kennedy is assassinated in Dallas, Texas; Vice-President Lyndon B. Johnson is sworn in as president.

1964—U.S. aircraft bomb North Vietnam. Johnson is elected president. Herbert Hoover dies in New York City.

1965—U.S. combat troops arrive in South Vietnam.

1966—Thousands protest U.S. policy in Vietnam. National Guard quells race riots in Chicago.

1967—Six-Day War between Israel and Arab nations.

1968—Martin Luther King, Jr., is assassinated in Memphis, Tennessee. Senator Robert Kennedy is assassinated in Los Angeles. Riots and police brutality take place at Democratic National Convention in Chicago. Richard Nixon is elected president. Czechoslovakia is invaded by Soviet troops.

1969—Dwight D. Eisenhower dies in Washington, D.C. Hundreds of thousands of people in several U.S. cities demonstrate against Vietnam War.

1970—Four Vietnam War protesters are killed by National Guardsmen at Kent State University in Ohio.

1971—Twenty-Sixth Amendment allows eighteen-year-olds to vote.

1972—Nixon visits Communist China; is reelected president in near-record landslide. Watergate affair begins when five men are arrested in the Watergate hotel complex in Washington, D.C. Nixon announces resignations of aides Haldeman, Ehrlichman, and Dean and Attorney General Kleindienst as a result of Watergate-related charges. Harry S. Truman dies in Kansas City, Missouri.

1973—Vice-President Spiro Agnew resigns; Gerald Ford is named vice-president. Vietnam peace treaty is formally approved after nineteen months of negotiations. Lyndon B. Johnson dies in San Antonio, Texas.

1974—As a result of Watergate cover-up, impeachment is considered; Nixon resigns and Ford becomes president. Ford pardons Nixon and grants limited amnesty to Vietnam War draft evaders and military deserters.

1975—U.S. civilians are evacuated from Saigon, South Vietnam, as Communist forces complete takeover of South Vietnam.

1976—U.S. celebrates its Bicentennial. James Earl Carter becomes president.

1977—Carter pardons most Vietnam draft evaders, numbering some 10,000.

1980—Ronald Reagan is elected president.

1981—President Reagan is shot in the chest in assassination attempt. Sandra Day O'Connor is appointed first woman justice of the Supreme Court.

1983—U.S. troops invade island of Grenada.

1984—Reagan is reelected president. Democratic candidate Walter Mondale's running mate, Geraldine Ferraro, is the first woman selected for vice-president by a major U.S. political party.

1985—Soviet Communist Party secretary Konstantin Chernenko dies; Mikhail Gorbachev succeeds him. U.S. and Soviet officials discuss arms control in Geneva. Reagan and Gorbachev hold summit conference in Geneva. Racial tensions accelerate in South Africa.

1986—Space shuttle *Challenger* explodes shortly after takeoff; crew of seven dies. U.S. bombs bases in Libya. Corazon Aquino defeats Ferdinand Marcos in Philippine presidential election.

1987—Iraqi missile rips the U.S. frigate *Stark* in the Persian Gulf, killing thirty-seven American sailors. Congress holds hearings to investigate sale of U.S. arms to Iran to finance Nicaraguan *contra* movement.

1988—President Reagan and Soviet leader Gorbachev sign INF treaty, eliminating intermediate nuclear forces. Severe drought sweeps the United States. George Bush is elected president.

1989—East Germany opens Berlin Wall, allowing citizens free exit. Communists lose control of governments in Poland, Romania, and Czechoslovakia. Chinese troops massacre over 1,000 pro-democracy student demonstrators in Beijing's Tiananmen Square.

1990—Iraq annexes Kuwait, provoking the threat of war. East and West Germany are reunited. The Cold War between the United States and the Soviet Union comes to a close. Several Soviet republics make moves toward independence.

1991—Backed by a coalition of members of the United Nations, U.S. troops drive Iraqis from Kuwait. Latvia, Lithuania, and Estonia withdraw from the USSR. The Soviet Union dissolves as its republics secede to form a Commonwealth of Independent States.

1992—U.N. forces fail to stop fighting in territories of former Yugoslavia. More than fifty people are killed and more than six hundred buildings burned in rioting in Los Angeles. U.S. unemployment reaches eight-year high. Hurricane Andrew devastates southern Florida and parts of Louisiana. International relief supplies and troops are sent to combat famine and violence in Somalia.

1993—U.S.-led forces use airplanes and missiles to attack military targets in Iraq. William Jefferson Clinton becomes the forty-second U.S. president.

1994—Richard M. Nixon dies in New York City.

Index

Page numbers in boldface type indicate illustrations.

About the Author

Zachary Kent grew up in Little Falls, New Jersey, and received an English degree from St. Lawrence University. Following college he worked at a New York City literary agency for two years and then launched his writing career. To support himself while writing, he has worked as a taxi driver, a shipping clerk, and a house painter. Mr. Kent has had a lifelong interest in American history. Studying the U.S. presidents was his childhood hobby. His collection of presidential items includes books, pictures, and games, as well as several autographed letters.